"Prioritizing people over things is a simple enough concept, but few organizations are really practicing it. *Move the Needle* is a timely reminder of why leaders need to put their personal purpose and their team above external results." - **Marshall Goldsmith, Thinkers 50 #1 Executive Coach and Only Two-time #1 Leadership Thinker in the World**

"Robb Holman takes readers on an engaging journey to learn how influence and leadership actually work. His Inside Out approach is rooted in wisdom, authenticity, and years of lived experience as a business leader and entrepreneur." - **Cy Wakeman, NY Times Bestselling Author & Global Thought Leader**

"This book was a great reminder of how acting from purpose is far more effective than acting from fear or the pressure to perform. Robb tells profound stories that demonstrate how personal conviction changes the game."- **Howard Behar, President of Starbucks, Retired**

"A brilliant follow-up to *All In*, this book provides grounded principles and concrete examples of how leading from the inside out can transform your organization's culture and reignite productivity. Robb's practical, heartfelt advice shows how simple actions yield massive results."- **Marcel Schwantes, Highly-Acclaimed Leadership Coach, Syndicated Business Columnist and Host of the *Love in Action* Podcast**

"Having purposeful leadership is essential for any organization's culture. This book gives practical steps to show teams how to lead from the inside out. Robb shares heart-servant leadership principles that every leader should learn to move the needle for peak performance in their team's development." - **Jasmine Romaine, Transformation Strategist, Global Woman Award Honoree and Bestselling author of *Speak to Profit: Speak with Confidence and Jazz Up Your Sales***

"Move the Needle: How Inside Out Leaders Influence Organizational Culture is a must read for any leader looking to make a transformational difference. Using a story-driven approach, Robb Holman expertly lays out the steps leaders must take to not only create organizations that flourish but organizations where employees live their very best life - not just through their work but because of the kind of culture they work in everyday. *Move the Needle* will transform your culture and your leadership."- **Dr. Brad Shuck, University of Louisville and Co-Founder, OrgVitals**

"Guiding leaders in connecting with others to help them reach their full potential is a tall order, but Robb's latest book helps leaders define real success while also presenting much-needed insights and modern knowledge for positive business results." - **Kari Mirabal, International Keynote and TEDx Speaker, Author, and Networking Consultant**

"Robb just gets it! *Move the Needle* gives a blueprint for strengthening team relationships, serving from the heart, and doing work that matters - a must-read. The questions for reflection provide grip to the principles in each chapter." - **Dan Rockwell, Inc Magazine Top 50 Leadership Expert**

"Effective leadership demonstrates that people and service matter most and creates a culture where these flourish. Robb easily and passionately communicates not only how to be an effective leader, but he also shows us how to nurture a culture that will raise up the leaders among us."- **Michelle Rouse Fox, Founder and CEO Foxygen Consulting**

"Through stories, Robb skillfully brings to life the power and benefits of a People First culture. I have found this to be part of the secret sauce in successful organizations."- **Lance Knaub, Founder Breakthru Physical Therapy + Fitness, Denali Consulting, Best Selling Author of *The 4% Break-Thru***

"*Move the Needle* guides us not only how to run a successful organization, but how to leave a potent legacy of your work in the process. Whether you're a leader with a title or a leader in spirit you will learn from this book" - **Ellen Rogin, author of the NY Times Bestseller Picture Your Prosperity**

"Some books take a long time to get to the point or at least to anything actionable. Move The Needle jumps right in with meaningful stories and poignant takeaways. Robb Holman does a FANTASTIC job of weaving in emotional content with practical systems you can use to uplevel your leadership quotient. Amazing work!" - **Robert Kennedy III, President, Kennetik Kommunications "We Help You Deliver Messages That Move Your People"**

"*Move the Needle* is a powerful reminder that at the end of the day, leaders need to prioritize people before things. Robb gives simple tips to make prioritization a daily practice, and he shows you how to create a culture people never want to leave." - **Justin Patton, Author of Bold New You**

MOVE THE NEEDLE

HOW INSIDE OUT LEADERS INFLUENCE ORGANIZATIONAL CULTURE

ROBB HOLMAN

means—

1-326-73437-4 (sc)
1-326-73436-7 (e)

October 9, 2021

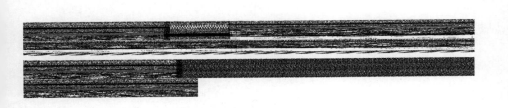

CONTENTS

Foreword   xi

I   xiv

PART I:

         1

         10

         19

         28

PART II:

         38

         47

         55

PART III:

         66

Ch   76

         85

         94

FOREWORD

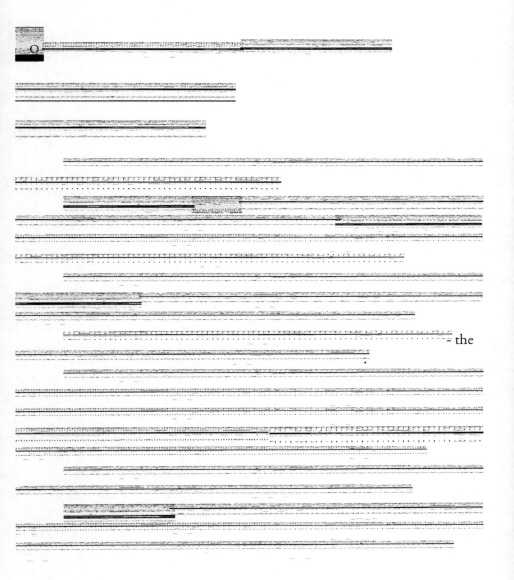

INTRODUCTION

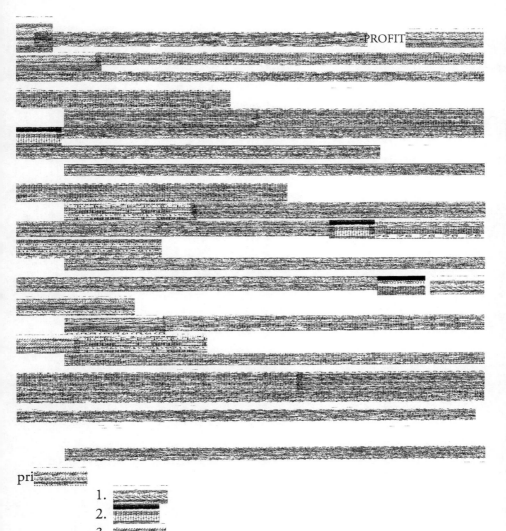

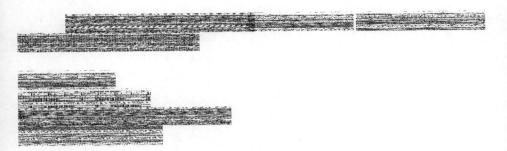

PART I

Purpose Principles

CHAPTER 1

Influence That Matters

"The key to successful leadership is influence, not authority." - Ken Blanchard

ONE FRIDAY NIGHT, my soon-to-be wife and I were watching a movie when the phone rang. I picked up, surprised to hear the voice of a young man I'd met just a week earlier. He sounded shaky and confused. It didn't take long to realize he was under the wrong kind of influence.

"Robb, I'm going to kill myself," he announced.

I felt paralyzed, imprisoned in fear.

At the time, our community church would invite visitors to receive prayer and counsel after the weekly sermons. I served on the team that facilitated this process, which is how I met this young man of about 18 years old. With tears streaming down his face, he had shared that he was addicted to drugs and alcohol and struggled with severe depression.

With each second that passed, he became more incoherent as he spoke over the phone. Time was of the essence. All I knew was that I cared for him

1

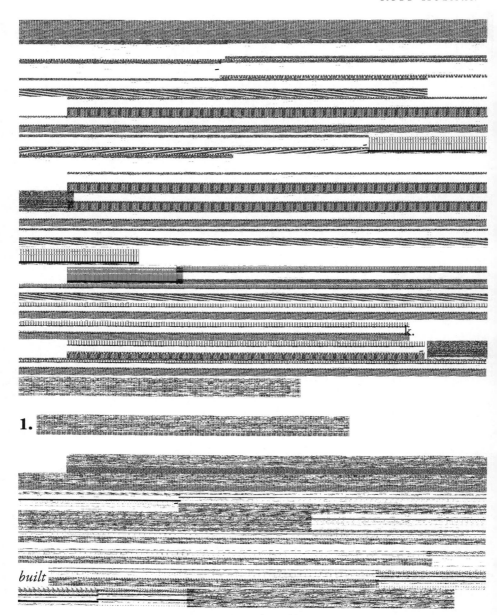

1.

built

1.
2. way.
3.
4.

5.

ntial

itself.

b

speak.

I w

1.
2.

1.
2. Treat
3.
4.

CHAPTER - 2

Purpose That Compels Action

"If you have a strong purpose in life, you don't have to be pushed. Your passion will drive you there." - Roy T. Bennett

INSIDE OUT LEADERS who move the needle toward greater organizational influence are purposeful in almost everything they do. There is a good reason for this: Their actions spring from a deep place.

I was recently on a coaching call with a leader who was considering a career transition. During the call, I could sense he wanted to get an amen from me so he could leverage his skills and kick off his plan of action. I told him it was important to know the reason behind the career pivot before moving forward. Initially, he gave a general, professional answer, only hinting at something far more personal.

I encouraged him to dig deeper, asking what motivated the career transition in the first place. His answer, while a bit more meaningful, wasn't quite what I was looking for.

As I coaxed him with more why questions throughout the conversation, he peeled back the layers toward his true purpose. His clear and concise awareness of how to solve a specific problem was illuminated. As a result of this knowledge, he was compelled to take action and start his own

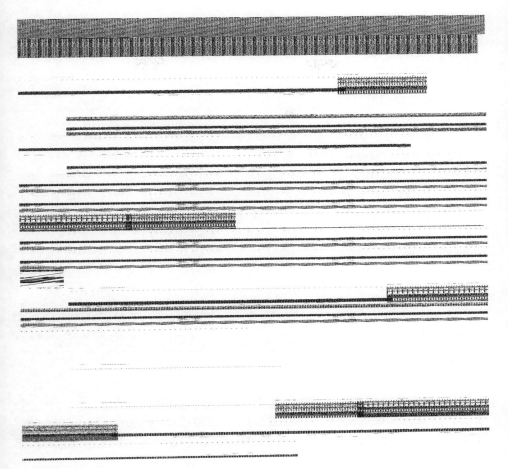

who

1.

2.

3.

4.
                                                              ng

5.

L

All

In

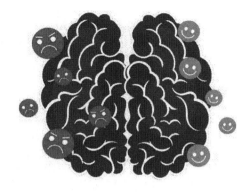

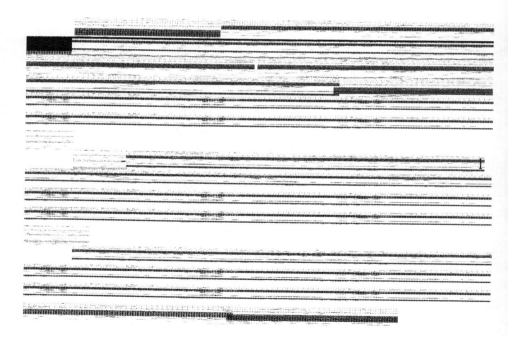

-

- Sp

will be

ve

, but

You

or s

1.

2.

3.

4.

-
-
-

days?

CHAPTER - 3

You Do What You Value

"Values reflect what is important to the way you live and work." - Glenn C. Stewart

I'LL NEVER FORGET THE TIMES MY DAD WOULD SAY, "We're going somewhere really fun, but I can't tell you until we get there!" As a kid, I'd immediately keel over with excitement and anticipation. Of course, I'd ask him where we were going a few times (or should I say a few thousand times) before we arrived at our destination.

Sometimes my dad knocked it out of the park. But more often than not, we were disappointed once the surprise was unveiled. Nonetheless, he was demonstrating the value of experience.

Recently, our family took a much-needed vacation to a lake house about 2 hours from home. We were smack in the middle of the Coronavirus pandemic, and everyone was getting a bit stir crazy.

On the second day of our trip, I decided to rent a boat and take the whole family around the lake to explore. The only problem was, I had never been the captain of a boat - only a passive spectator.

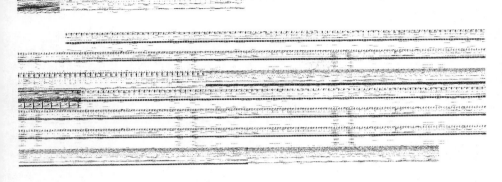

All In

living

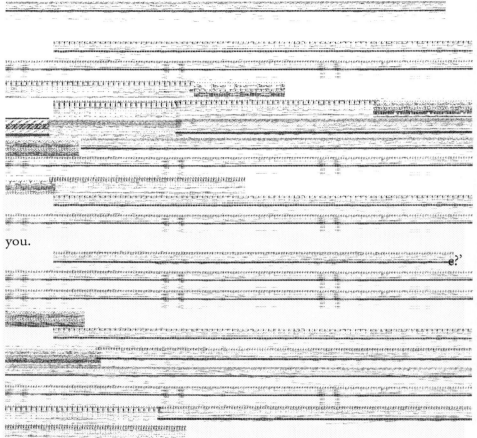

you.

e?"

sing

us to

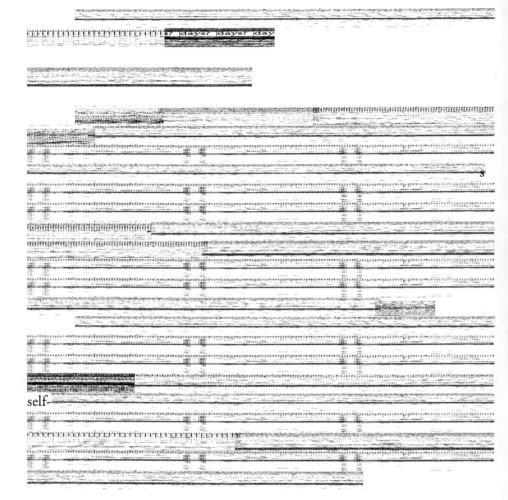

self-

BOUNDED SET   CENTERED SET

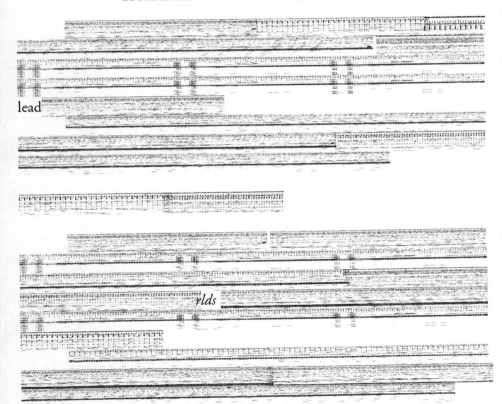

lead

rlds

from-

from-

and

and and and

limits

fear   choice.

empo

26

The

1.
2.
3. o do

-
-
-

CHAPTER 4

Simplicity That Ensures Outcomes

"Live simply that others might simply live."
— Elizabeth Seaton

A FEW YEARS AGO, a good friend and leader told me he wanted to give away all of his possessions and go serve in an underprivileged country. Although he was motivated from the heart to do so, this was not the main reason. Admittedly, he had accumulated a growing business with growing problems. He saw this drastic change as a chance to escape.

We often think that escapes are entry points to a simpler life. But this is an outside-in strategy. A better and lasting solution is learning to simplify our lives right here, right now. That's the inside out approach.

I know what you might be thinking: What does this have to do with influencing organizational culture? Hang in there!

My friend realized that his life had become too complex. He was drowning in the details of his situation. From this space of feeling trapped, he figured, "If this is what it's going to be, then I'm out of here."

7).

gilds

-on-one.

you

1.

over- deli

to.

to

1.
2.
3.

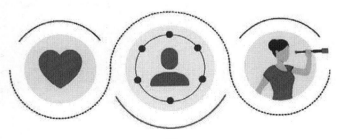

in;

too.

g

you *you*

it.

This

you *you*

infl

1.
2.
3.

4.

-
-
-

PART II

People Principles

CHAPTER - 5

People Before Things

"It's not what we have in life, but who we have in our life that matters." - J.M. Laurence

PURPOSE IS THE FOUNDATION we must build upon. So far, we've learned 4 purpose principles that will prepare you for greater success:

1. Influence that matters
2. Purpose that compels action
3. We do what we value
4. Simplicity that ensures outcomes

As we act on these principles, we influence those around us more purposefully. This next section is all about building relationships from the inside out.

people

their

Inside

Thi

The Corporate "Caste System"

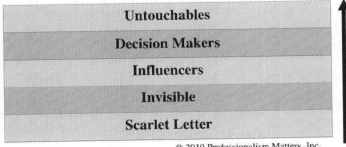

Untouchables

Decision Makers

Influencers

Invisible

Scarlet Letter

Organizational Power

3

1.

2.

3.

real-

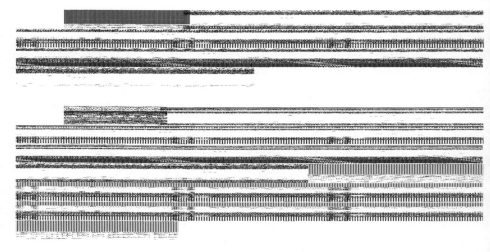

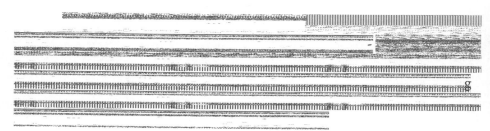

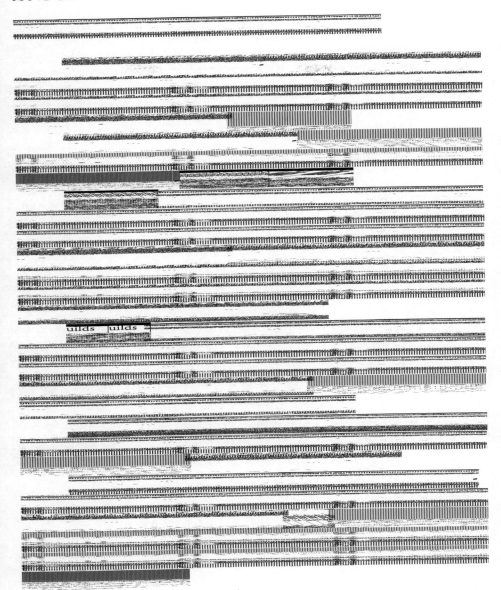

1.
2.
3.
4.

-
-
-

CHAPTER - 6

Serving: Leadership That Empowers

"The true heroes of the new millennium will be servant leaders, quietly working out of the spotlight to transform our world."
- Ann McGee-Cooper

ONCE YOU EMBRACE team members for who they are rather than what they can do for you and the organization, opportunities for service are revealed.

Inside Out leaders proactively seek ways to serve their team members. When I wrote this chapter, we were in lockdown. The Coronavirus was impacting people, businesses, and our entire culture in the US and throughout the world.

There's no doubt that the pandemic disrupted my personal life. Keynote talks were canceled, there was uncertainty around my wife's job, and my 3 children, normally in public schools, were suddenly being homeschooled.

I heard so much speculation about the impact the virus would have on our lives. Opinions were all over the spectrum. Some people sat at the extremes, while others had oscillating thoughts and feelings. Some were caught

the vi

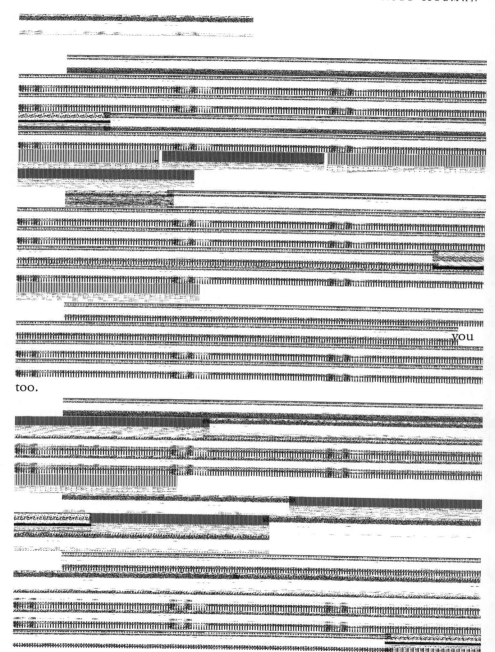

you

too.

Treat

Oft

lead.

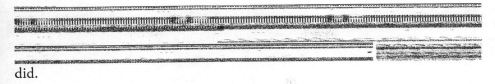

did.

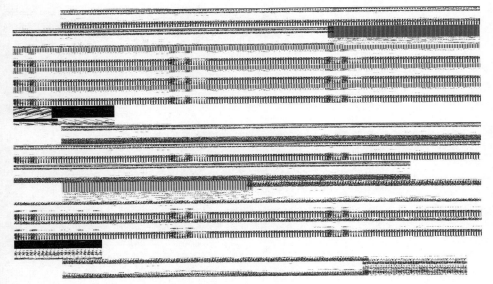

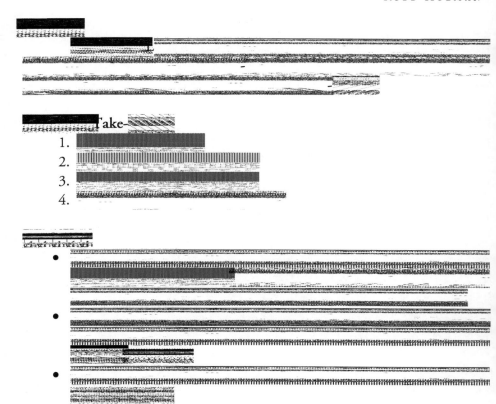

CHAPTER - 7

Influence That Inspires

"I've learned that people will forget what you said, people will forget what you did, but people will never forget how you made them feel."
- Maya Angelou

Aᴛ ᴛʜɪs ᴘᴏɪɴᴛ, ʏᴏᴜ ᴍɪɢʜᴛ ʙᴇ ᴛʜɪɴᴋɪɴɢ, "As an organizational leader, I never signed up to be a therapist!"

Don't worry. You don't need to be a therapist. All you need to learn is presence and authentic engagement.

While leaders empower people through service, one invaluable thing that keeps that power alive is having influence that inspires. Moving the needle is about inspiring people with an idea while taking incremental steps to arrive at the destination together. Essentially, the big victory is found in the small ones.

A few years ago, I was facilitating a leadership training workshop. My goal was to stretch the group beyond its comfort zone. The beauty of this particular workshop was that I knew everyone in attendance. It was an extremely diverse group in upbringing, ethnicity, and worldview. Many were used to swimming in their own lane and hanging out with like-minded people.

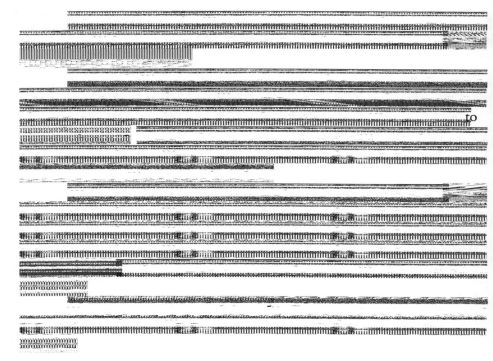

to

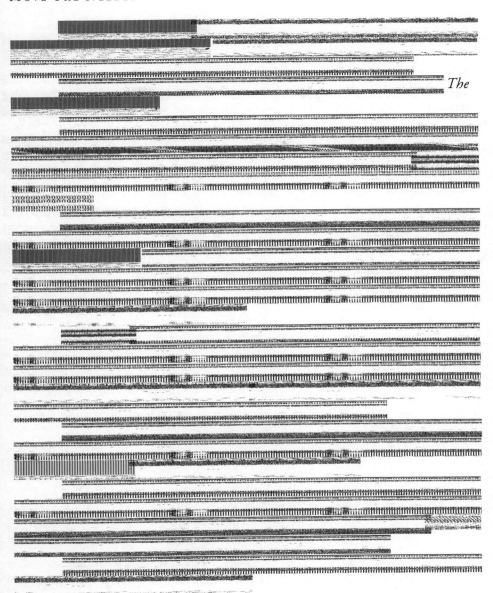

The

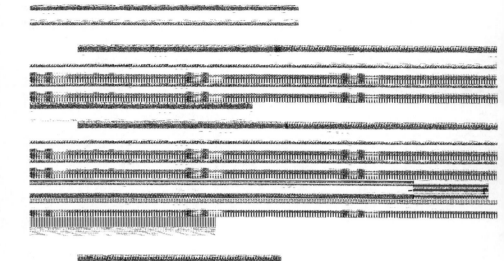

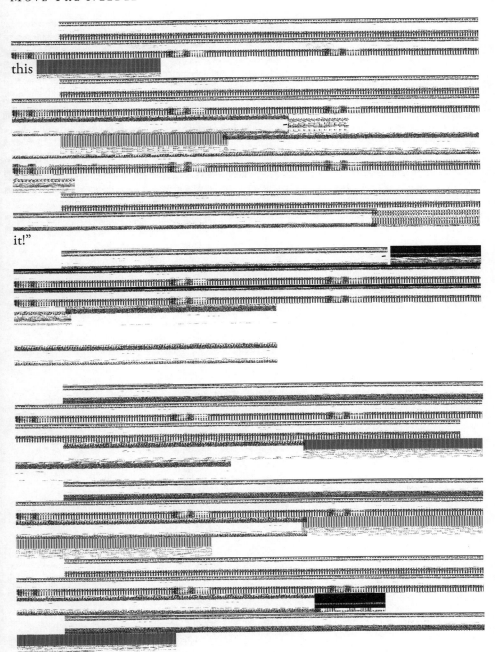

this

it!"

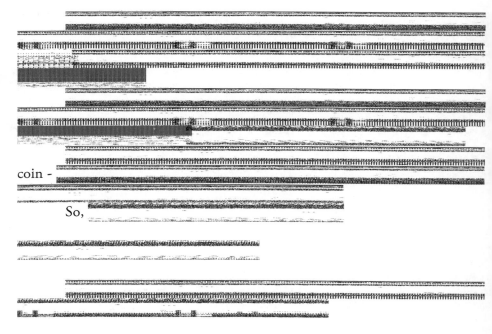

coin -

So,

Most Employees Experience Burnout at Work

Please indicate how often the following is true for your job: You feel burned out at work.

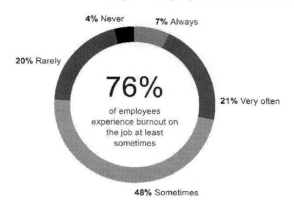

4% Never

7% Always

20% Rarely

76%
of employees
experience burnout on
the job at least
sometimes

21% Very often

48% Sometimes

GALLUP

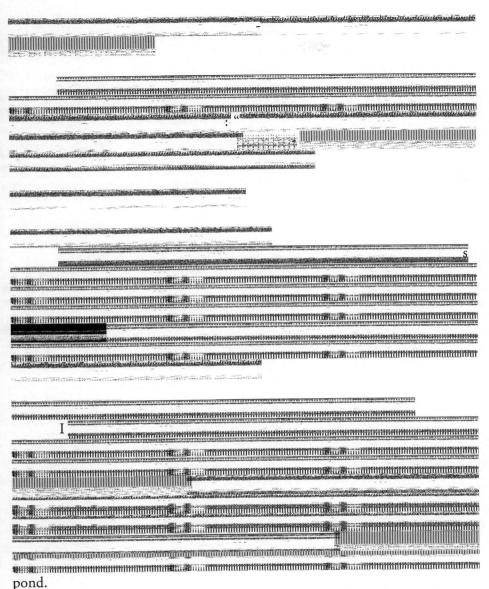

pond.

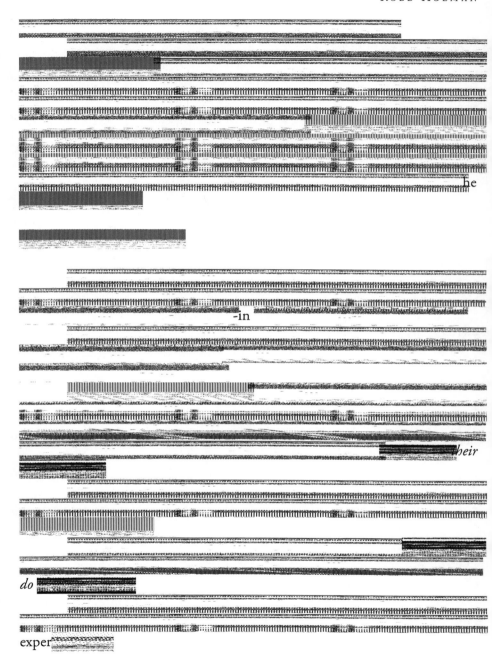

he

-in

their

do

exper

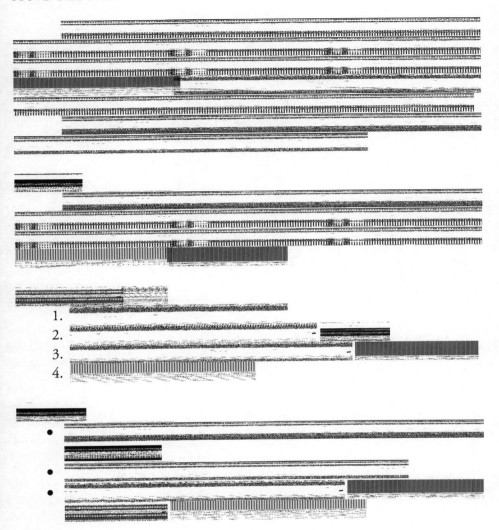

PART III

Process Principles

CHAPTER - 8

Efficiency Through Effectiveness

"Efficiency is doing things right; effectiveness is doing the right things."
- Peter Drucker

SOMETIMES PROCESSES ARE EFFICIENT, but the organization is doing the wrong thing. We can't fool ourselves into thinking that good activity is always the best activity. Efficiency through effectiveness is doing *the right thing the right way.*

Years ago, I was the CEO of a basketball clothing company called Push the Rock Outfitters. I enjoyed going on sales tours each year, taking our latest basketball gear, and talking to college coaches in the northeastern US.

Oftentimes, I'd call my wife on the way home, excited to tell her about the coaches and the wonderful conversations we had about our lives and families. I thought I was doing the right thing in the right way. My wife would often ask if I acquired any new business from the trips. To be honest, I was just thankful to be growing my relationships with these people. I'll never forget the day I returned from what seemed like a great sales trip and my wife asked, "Did you end up getting a business deal?"

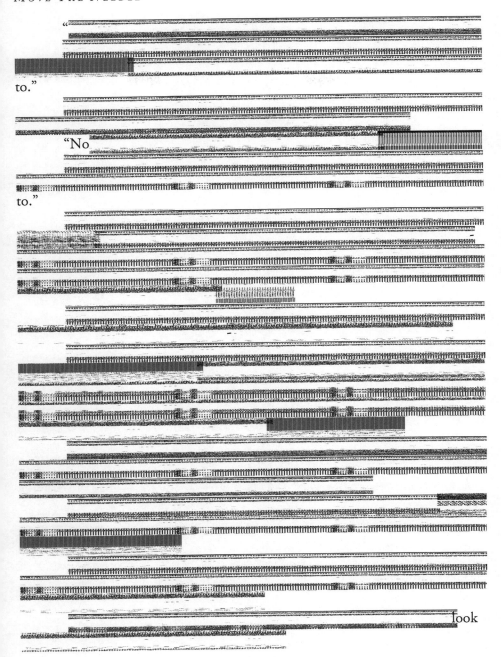

"

to."

"No

to."

look

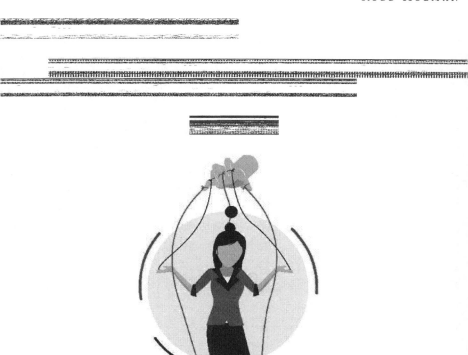

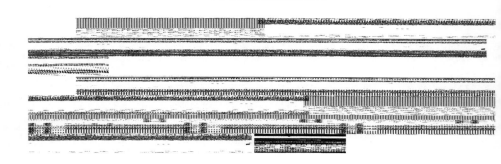

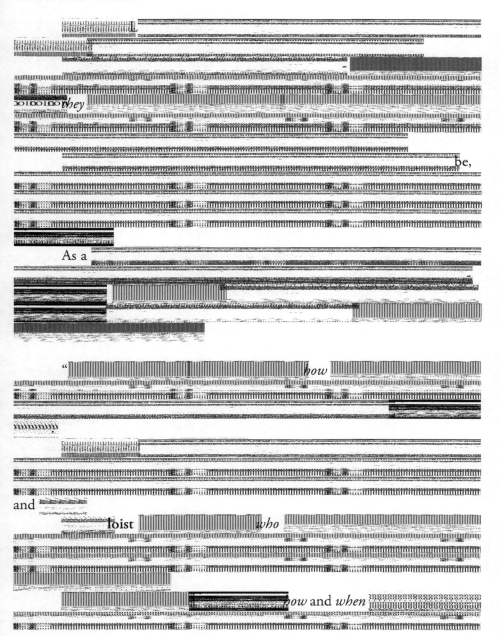

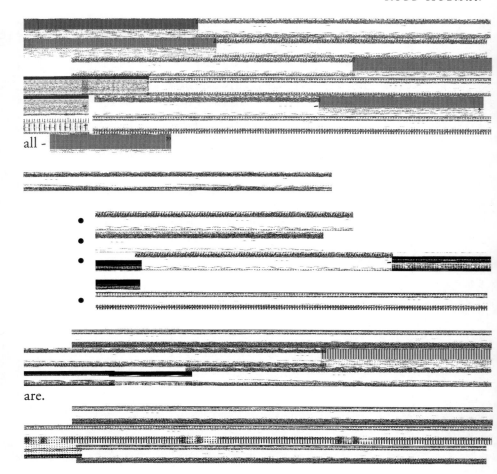

all -

are.

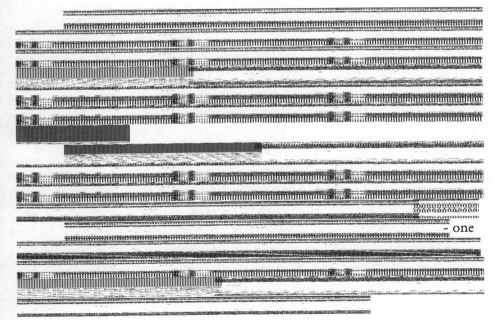

- one

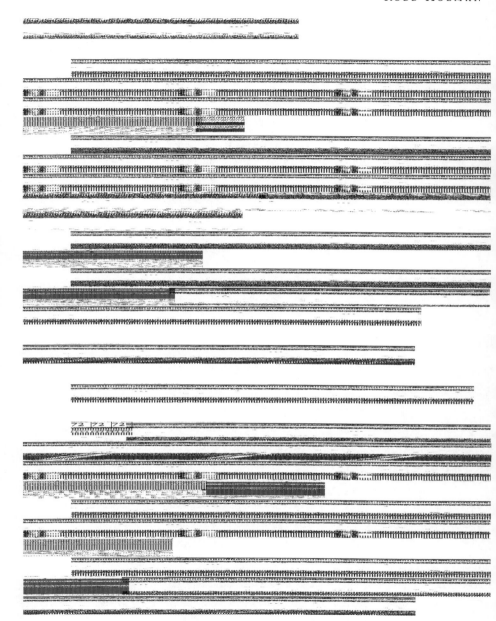

you

- the

gives

keeps

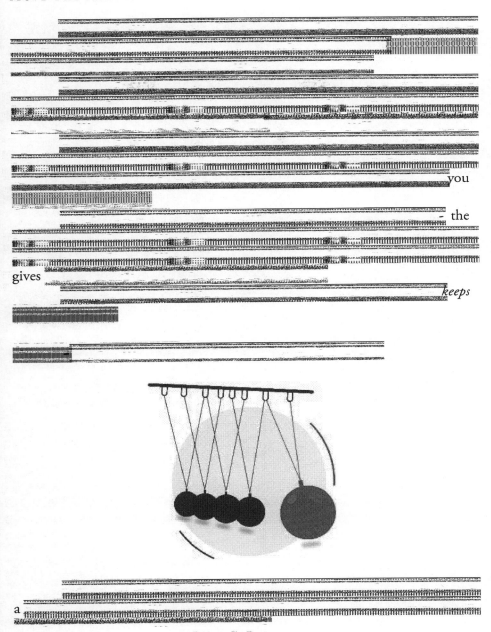

a

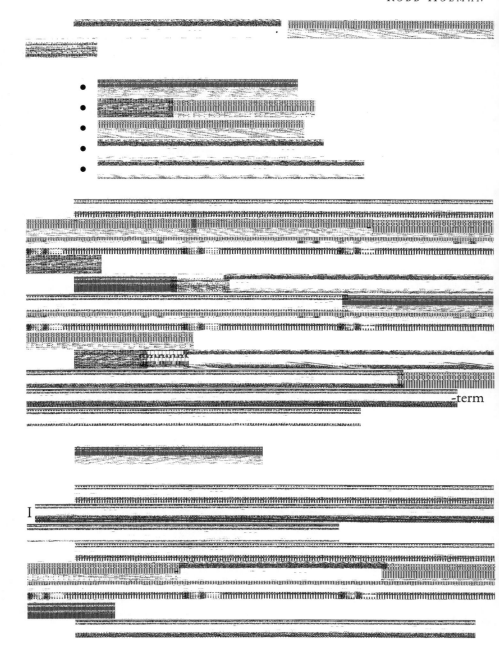

-term

I

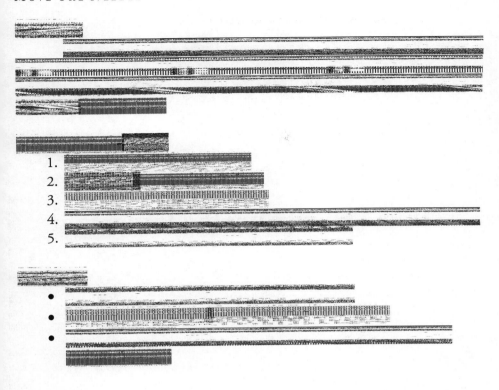

1.
2.
3.
4.
5.

CHAPTER - 9

Time: Prioritizing the Important

*"Three things you cannot recover in life: the words after they're said,
the moment after it's missed, and the time after it's gone."*
- Anonymous

As far back as I can remember, I've always been good at time management.

In college, when my friends and classmates were pulling all-nighters cramming for a big test, I was sleeping soundly. This used to drive them crazy! To this day, I can count on one hand how many times I've stayed up all night - at least intentionally. It's a good thing, as lack of sleep is one of my greatest vulnerabilities.

As we discussed in the last chapter, utilizing deadlines effectively is key. I have always kept the end in mind, planning backward with a timeline of accomplishing goals.

For instance, when I prepare a keynote talk, I typically begin the heavy lifting about one month before the presentation. Even before then, I do some minor research on the audience, etc.

When I prepare far in advance, this allows me to be free in thought and emotion as I get closer to the talk. I always know that I'm fully prepared

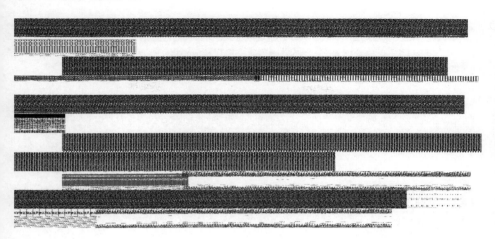

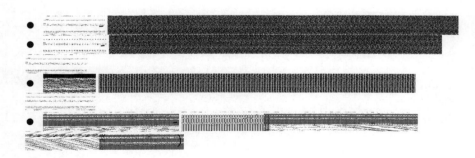

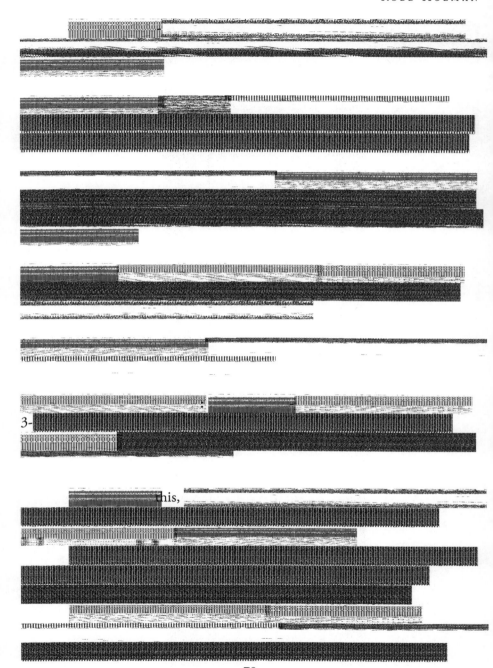

3-

this,

exac

and

areareare

rest.

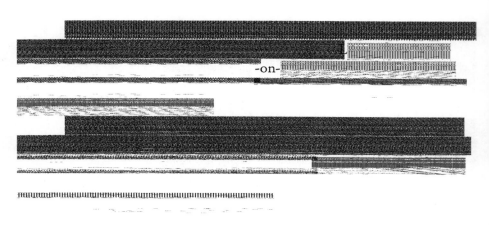

In ▓▓▓▓▓▓▓▓▓▓▓best-

a 60-

-whe

are

tion,

work

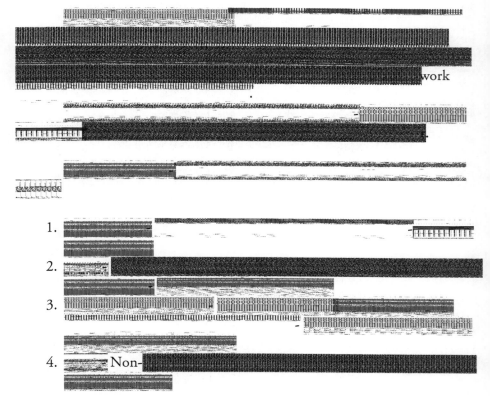

1.

2.

3.

4. Non-

inve

CHAPTER - 10

Leaving a Legacy

"Carve your name on hearts, not
tombstones. A legacy is etched into the
minds of others and the stories they share
about you." - Shannon L. Alder

ALMOST 25 YEARS after my college basketball team celebrated one of the best records in its history, a conference championship, and #1 seed in the NCAA Tournament, I finally reconnected with my team.

I came across a former teammate's Facebook post and thought it might be a good idea to get together, reminisce, and catch up. So, I made a closed Facebook group and hunted down everyone who was on the roster that magical season.

Sure enough, I managed to find everyone and strike up a conversation in the group. I was blown away by the transparency, encouragement, and laughter. One former teammate even shared something that he had kept inside for more than 20 years.

It's easy to forget the impact a leader can have on their team after years of being apart. But this is what leaving a legacy is all about. Moving the needle means becoming a gardener. Leaders plant and water seeds that one

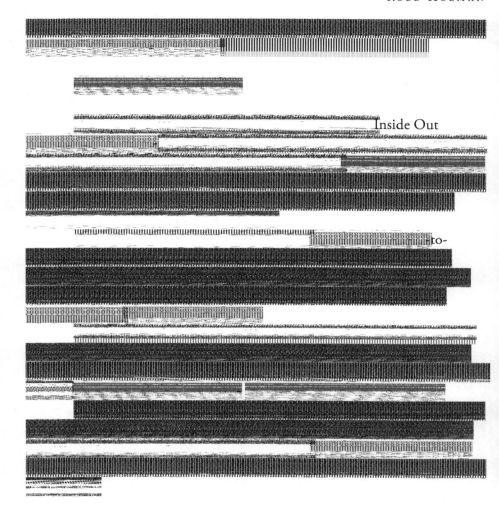

Inside Out

-to-

Inside Out

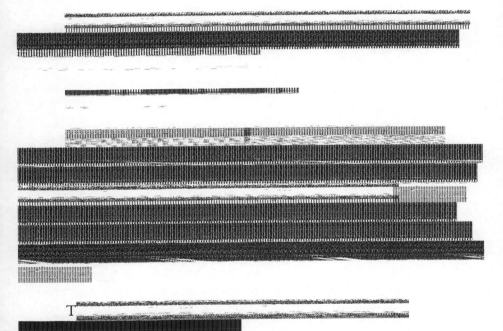

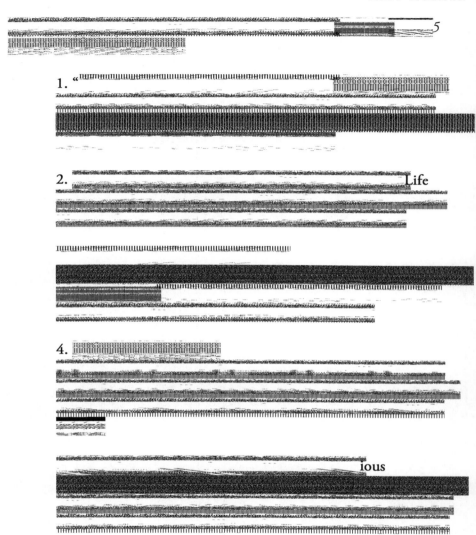

-to-

- tasks?

- rs?

-

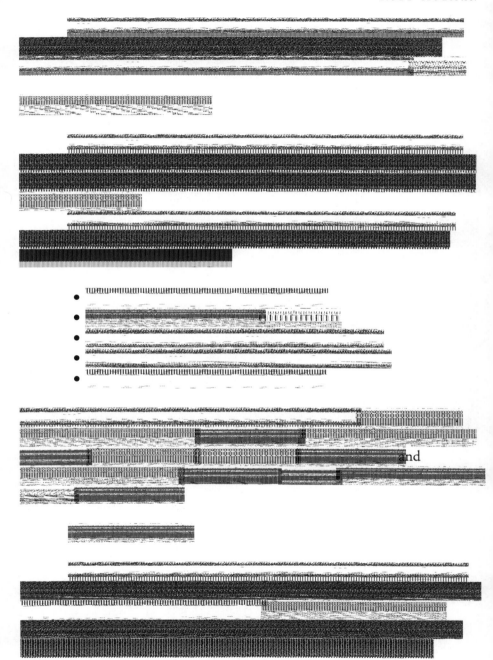

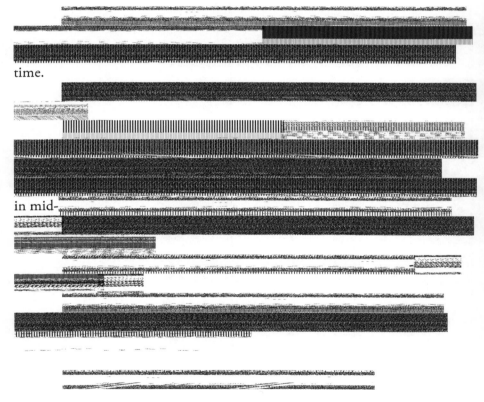

time.

in mid-

you?

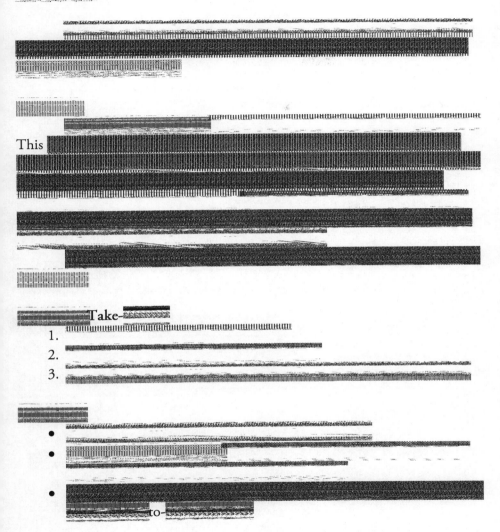

This

Take-

1.

2.

3.

to-

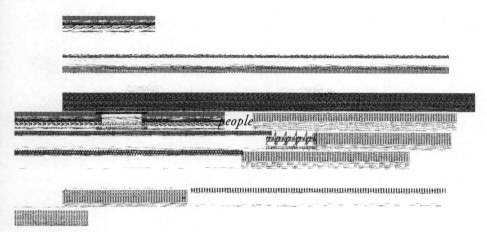

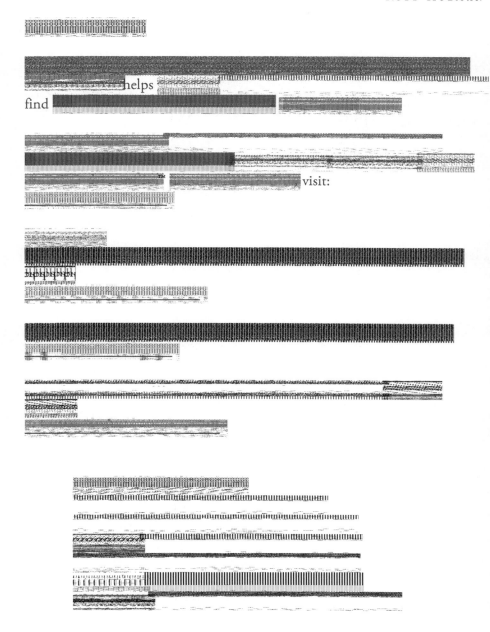

helps

find

visit:

POSITIVE. PASSIONATE. POWERFUL.

RH ROBB HOLMAN
INSIDE OUT LEADERSHIP

ROBB HOLMAN

is an internationally recognized leadership expert, executive coach, keynote speaker, podcast co-host, and bestselling author who has a heart for authentic relationships and a true talent for equipping people with the skills and the knowledge necessary for their success. His work has been featured in top publications like Inc., Forbes, and Fast Company and endorsed by many of the world's top leadership thinkers.

http://www.robbholman.com/speaking

 Robb.holman

 Robbholman1

 Robbholman

 @Robbholman

> *Robb is a charismatic and dynamic speaker who has the ability to capture an audience from the moment he speaks. You can tell by his presence the passion he has for his business and his leadership. I would highly recommend Robb for any speaking engagements. The take-away knowledge and inspiration for your audience is abundant.*
>
> — **Carla Haydt**

 www.robbholman.com　　 484.401.7966　　 info@robbholman.com

ABOUT THE BOOK

Internationally recognized leadership expert reveals his secrets for lasting leadership success to help you LEAD the WAY.

http://leadthewaybook.com/

www.robbholman.com

484.401.7966

info@robbholman.com

ABOUT THE BOOK

All In takes leaders on a inspirational and practical journey of learning how to build trust from the inside out. When trust is built and fostered, teams can accomplish the impossible together!

getallinbook.com

www.robbholman.com

484.401.7966

info@robbholman.com

To Take The

Inside Out Leadership™ Check-Up *Visit:*

www.leadthewaybook.com/jointhemovement

Sign In

Using This Passcode.

LTW17RJH

This passcode is good for one person only.

http://www.robbholman.com

info@robbholman.com

Made in the USA
Middletown, DE
27 October 2021

51125708R00068